EXCEL

MACROS

Programming For Complete Beginners, Step-By-Step Illustrated Guide to Master Excel Macros

Copyright © 2018 by William B. Skates

Complementary Book

Excel VBA: Programming for Complete Beginners

Introduction

Getting Started!

Hello, there future Excel Programmers! The aim of this book is to provide complete information about the Macros in excel. Starting from the very basic explanation of Macros, we will dig deeper, step by step in each chapter briefly detailing all the important properties of Macros and what you need to know to get started in this domain.

A very disciplined approach is taken for writing this book which will be very easy for readers to understand, who we assume are very new to this topic. We will explore all the areas relating to Macros and will also go in to the VBA(Visual Basic for applications). We will also mention some important techniques for recording Macros and how Macros are actually stored in excel(Which format?).

After reading this book, the reader will have complete knowledge about Macros, VBA(Visual Basic for Applications), the relationship between VBA and Macros, what is the difference between Absolute Macro recording and Relative Macro Recording, what are VBA Excel Objects, how to send an e-mail directly from Microsoft excel and a dedicated chapter defining a complete approach for debugging. Apart from this many other small level details will also be explained, so that our reader doesn't feel the need to google anything and deviate from the actual topic.

Chapter 1: What are Macros?

Macros

A macro is basically a program/action which is a replacement for recurring mouse or keyboard actions in Microsoft Excel. Macros are used to help save the time of users by automating some repetitive tasks that you have to do over and over again. In Excel, creating a Macro which is also termed as recording a macro is done using Macro recorder. The recorded Macros are written in Visual basic for Applications(VBA). For now, you only need to know that VBA is a programming language which is used for creating Macros. Since Excel is a Microsoft product, VBA is also developed by Microsoft.

More brief definition of a Macro

Now you have a basic idea about Macros. You know that they are written in VBA, but how can a person specifically define a Macro to a professional person. For example, you cannot say that Macro is a VBA. We all know Macros are written in VBA but professionally the correct way to define a Macro to a technical person or programmer is: "Macros are Visual Basic procedures that are used to automate tasks in Excel, saving users time and efforts".

Macro Recorder

One way of creating Macros is by writing instructions or by coding directly in VBA editor. This approach is used by developers who are properly aware of Macros and are familiar with coding to a great extent.

Another approach is used to generate VBA code automatically. This approach is useful for novice users who are not familiar about coding or syntax of the VBA. This approach is achieved through Macro Recorder. As you interact with data in the excel, the Macro recorder examines your actions and them automatically generates VBA code respectively.

For further convenience, we can link the macros to different keyboard shortcuts. In this way, the keyboard shortcuts will act as commands for triggering a Macro.

Is Macro Recorder enough for all our automation needs?

Now, one might ask, if you have Macro Recorder, what is the purpose of manually giving instructions for a Macro in a VBA editor? The answer to this is very simple but is of immense importance if you want to know about significance of coding in Macros: There are certain functionalities which Macro Recorder cannot record or provide automatically. For example, Macro Recorder cannot provide loop functions and screen prompts. To achieve this functionality, you need to code in VBA editor.

Chapter 2: Getting Started with VBA

VBA (Visual Basic for Applications)

VBA is a programming language that is developed by Microsoft, in Excel the Macros are programmed in this language. So, it is very important for you to know about VBA because you will be spending most of the time coding Macros in this language.

Now before moving further, you should know that the VBA is not limited or restricted to Microsoft Excel only, it is also very consistently used with applications like MS-word and MS-Access(Microsoft's own database Application).

What can you do with VBA?

Some tasks require complex calculations which cannot be satisfied with in-built functions of Excel. This is where VBA plays its part, you can write set of instructions for performing calculations and create Macros comprising of these instructions. You can use these Macros again and again as long as it satisfies your needs. This would not be possible without the ability to build customize Macros.

Creating custom commands, new spreadsheet functions and functions for performing repetitive and frequent actions, all of this can be done by coding Macros using VBA.

Using the VBA

As mentioned before, all of the coding is done in VBA editor. To open VBA editor from Excel,

just press 'Alt+F11' and a new window will
open as shown in the figure below:

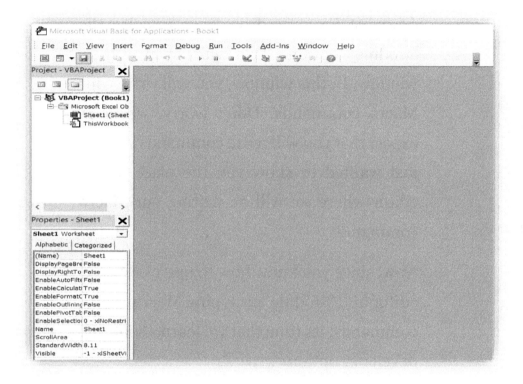

This is where you will write your Macros. When inside VBA editor, click on 'insert'. Few options will be displayed in a drop-down list. From the drop-down list select the 'Module' option. This will open a new window. In this window, you will write your Macro commands. Don't worry, we don't expect that you will write commands yet. We just wanted to show you the place in the editor where we will be writing our Macro commands.

Now, since you know how to open VBA editor and 'Module' for typing Macro commands, its time that we learn about the developer option.

The developer option

Before we start programming in VBA, we need to do one more step: Enable the Developer option. To do this, follow these steps:

1. Open a workbook in Excel.

2. Right click on the ribbon inside Excel workbook.

3. Click on customize ribbon.

4. Check the developer option.

As you can see in the picture given below, we have checked the developer option.

Shortcut for opening VBA editor

Earlier we showed you a shortcut for opening VBA editor, a different way, which takes couple of more steps, is to click on the 'developer' in the workbook ribbon, then click on the Visual Basic button, resulting in the opening of new window in VBA editor.

(Shortcut: Alt+F11)

Examples of function procedures

Here we shall look at the method of writing function procedures. Function procedures are very helpful in VBA code as they can be written to return a value and can be called as many times as you like.

To write a function we use the reserved keyword "Function" followed by a user-given name. An argument can also be passed to the function. An argument is basically a parameter with which we can interact with inside the function body to generate some useful result.

For example:

Function sum(a, b)

sum = a+b

End function

The function in the above code takes two parameters 'a' and 'b', adds them and stores the result in a variable called Sum.

With the above example, you must have had an idea about importance of function parameters. You can pass as much as **255** arguments to a function or you can pass non. That's right, you can even write a function without giving an argument.

Example of sub-procedure

Referring to an object inside the sub-procedure

Excel VBA contains a very interesting function called "HasFormula". This "HasFormula" lets you know that whether a specific cell inside the excel workbook contains a formula or not. If the cell contains a formula, it returns true, otherwise it returns false.

```
Sub check ()
Dim checkFormula As Boolean
```

```
checkFormula =
Range("B1:B2").HasFormula
MsgBox checkFormula
End Sub
```

In the above check() sub procedure, first of all we defined a variable with 'checkFormula' type 'Boolean' and then used '.HasFormula' with the Range("B1:B2") which returns true or false depending on whether or not the cells **B1** and **B2** contain a value or not. MsgBox is another function which is used for displaying values.

Referring to property of the object 'Columns'

We shall study about Excel objects in detail in the chapter 6. We shall write a function that sets the value of a specific range to "", i.e. It clears the contents of a particular range.

```
Function clearRange()

Columns.("A:A").clear

End Function
```

The second line in the above function clear the contents of the cell : "A".

Chapter 3: Macro Security

At this stage, you have a basic concept about Macros and VBA. In this book, we will be moving very slowly towards more advanced topics, addressing all the aspects of every single topic.

Macro security is very easy yet very sensitive topic. The reason it is considered sensitive is because if not understood properly it can be dangerous for your computer because without proper security you can get viruses through Macros, which ultimately can take the control of your whole computer and can harm your privacy.

Security settings

Inside Excel workbook under the 'developer', there is an option called 'Macro Security'. Click on the 'Macro Security, and a new window will appear with a list of options. The name of this window is Trust Center, highlighted as shown below.

Trusted Locations

In 'Trust Locations', all of your trusted locations for opening files will be listed. If you want to add a new location, always make sure that the new location is trustable and secure. Otherwise you can get dangerous malware and viruses from unknown sources. Never add unknown location for opening files, if you want to have a secure and computer-friendly environment (who doesn't want it).

Storing macros in your Personal Macro Workbook

To store the Macros in your personal Macro Workbook, first you need to create a Macro. To create a Macro go to 'Developer' tab. Under the 'Developer' tab click on 'Record Macro'. You will be asked to type in the name for your Macro to save in the workbook as shown in the figure below.

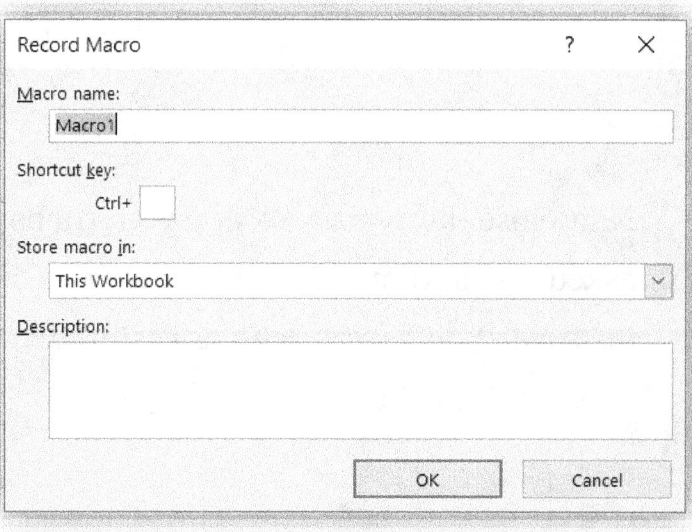

Record Macro	?	×
Macro name:		
Macro1		
Shortcut key:		
Ctrl+		
Store macro in:		
This Workbook		
Description:		
	OK	Cancel

You will see a text field as shown in the figure above that says, "This workbook". Since we want to store the macro in our personal workbook, we will click on the list for it to drop down. Then click on Personal Macro Workbook and then press 'OK'. Now as the name is set we shall perform actions which we want to store in the Personal Macro Workbook. After that click on Stop Recording under the 'Developer' tab as shown in the figure given below.

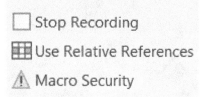

Now close this workbook and you will be asked if you want to save the changes. Click on 'save'. You have successfully stored Macro to your Personal Workbook.

Macro settings

Another very important option inside the trusted window is 'Macro settings'. This option gives you variety of choices as shown below in the figure:

Now we will explain the options in Macro settings:

Disable all Macros with notification

With this option Macros will be disabled, but you will be alerted if there are any security notifications regarding Macros that are present.

Disable all Macros without notification

All the security notifications and all the Macros are disabled with this option

Disable all Macros except digitally signed Macros

Macros are disabled, but if the Macros is signed by a trusted published then it will run.

Enable all Macros (not recommended)

With this option you can run all types of Macros whether trusted or not. This setting is usually not recommended as it makes our machine vulnerable to viruses and malware software.

Chapter 4: Recording your first Macro

If you have understood the VBA then this is just piece of cake for you. Recording the Macro doesn't mean that you will write the code in VBA and it will show the output in Excel workbook. The latter is true that the output will be showed in the Excel workbook, but prior is partially true. We said partially because ultimately VBA code is responsible for Macro behavior, but you will not write it. It will be automatically written.

Steps to record your first Macro

Now before we start, we would like to mention something here, the steps we follow will create a Macro which will do a task we want Excel to do. You can follow any steps you want as long as you understand the concept(how to record and use Macro).

1. Go to 'developers' tab.

2. Click on 'Record Macro'

3. When the Macro has been clicked, any action you perform will be monitored by Excel and will be converted to VBA code.

4. In this example, we will be determining Annual pay of person. We will use a formula called 'product' which you all are aware of: It multiplies two quantities.

5. While the Macro is recording, we will perform steps as shown in the figure given below.

◢	A	B	C	D	E
1	Monthly pay				
2	20000				
3	Annual Pay				
4	240000				
5					
6					
7					

6. After we have performed these steps, we will stop recording and save our macro.

7. Create a shortcut for your Macro. The shortcut will be of your choice, so you can choose any shortcut. For this example, we will be choosing 'Ctrl+c' as our shortcut key for calling our Macro.

Running a Macro

Once we have saved the Macro, now we can call the Macro using our shortcut key. As soon as we shall press 'Ctrl+c', all the steps you did while recording Macro will be repeated and you will see the output on the Excel sheet.

We mentioned earlier that all of the moves that you do while recording Macro are converted to VBA code. So, where is this VBA code? This VBA code is stored in Module.

As shown below, following are the lines that were generated while I was performing steps during Macro Recording.

```
Book1 - Module1 (Code)
(General)                                                    Calculate_yearly

Sub Calculate_yearly()
'
' Calculate_yearly Macro
'
' Keyboard Shortcut: Ctrl+c
'
    Range("A1").Select
    ActiveCell.FormulaR1C1 = "Monthly pay"
    Range("A2").Select
    ActiveCell.FormulaR1C1 = "20000"
    Range("A3").Select
    ActiveCell.FormulaR1C1 = "Annual Pay"
    Range("A4").Select
    ActiveCell.FormulaR1C1 = "=PRODUCT(R[-2]C,12)"
End Sub
```

The above window shows the operations performed during Recording converted to VBA commands. Two words are highlighted, these show the name of the Macro. Active Cell refers the current cell where pointer is pointing.

Assigning a macro to a button

Follow these steps to create your first Macro and assign it to a button:

1. Inside the 'developer' Tab, click on insert.

2. Click on the button as shown below.

3. Then left-click once, then should be able to see a button as follows:

	A	B	C	D	E	F	G	H
1								
2								
3								
4								
5							CommandButt	
6								
7								
8								
9								

4. Right-click on by keeping the mouse arrow on the button.

5. Select properties.

6. Select the name of the button and its caption. What you write in the caption will appear on the button.

7. As an example, here is the name and caption of my button.

8. Now left-click on the button twice and a new window will open in VBA editor. This is where you can code yourself in the sub-procedure which will take the commands. For example, you can write the code that what happens when you click the button. This is just one of the possibilities, you can make it perform several other tasks as well. Again, it all depends on you, you can write code according to your needs.

9. Add any command, for your learning, I have added a simple command which will

show a message "This button is clicked", whenever anyone clicks the button.

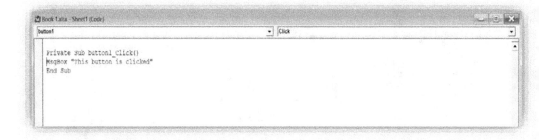

10. Now if you have created a button and want to delete, whatever the reason, you can do so easily by clicking on the 'design mode' under the 'developer' and then selecting the button and pressing the following keyboard

button "delete". There you go, button deleted.

After following all these steps, you have successfully created your first Macro. It was easy, wasn't it? If you keep following all the steps systematically and keep learning patiently then you will be able to master all Macro techniques easily.

Saving a Macro-Enabled Work Book

When we work with Macros inside the Excel, we need to save the workbook in a Macro-enabled format. The reason for this is that it provides an added security from external threats. To do that first we have to click on 'file' tab on the top left of the screen. Now if you move down some options you will see an option that says, "save as". Click on it and then you will be asked to select the location for saving the macro. Choose any location according to your need or priority. Once you have selected a location, click on the drop-down list as shown in figure below.

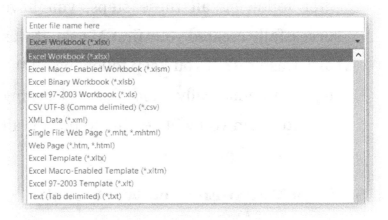

Click on the format that says, 'Excel Macro-Enabled Workbook(*.xlsm)'. You have successfully saved a Macro enabled file.

Chapter 5: Absolute vs. Relative Macro Recording

If you performed the Macro Recording activity in the "Recording your first Macro", you may have noticed that no matter how many time you run the Macro it always occupied the first four rows. It didn't matter where you pointed in the Excel worksheet, no matter which cell you are pointing, whenever we ran the Macro, it filled first four rows. Now, this is approach might not be effective as in worksheet you have to deal with large amounts of data and therefore, you can not keep the number of rows fixed. You may have to work on 1000's of rows or may be even more. We need something that can put data relative to previous data. This is where the concept of Relative and Absolute Macro recording steps in. Here we will briefly explain both approaches and guide you which approach is the best one.

Absolute Macro Recording

In absolute Macro Recording, actual references of the cells are recorded. This means whenever you will run the Macro with absolute references it will affect the fixed references only. Those fixed references are the references provided while you were recording Macro. Affection of the fixed reference means actual cells are affected every time whenever you run Macro.

Relative Macro Recording

In Relative Macro Recording, it doesn't matter which cell references you interact with during the Macro Recording. When you will run the Macro after saving it, it will affect those cells which you are pointing to currently or it will affect cells relatively from original cells.

Which approach is best?

Without a doubt Relative Macro recording is feasible for us because absolute Macro recording is of no use as it keeps updating the same cells again and again. Relative in the other hand affects cells relatively. It doesn't keep updating or writing the same cells again and again. So, the choice is easy, Relative Macro Recording is more helpful compare to Absolute Macro Recording.

How to perform Relative Macro Recording?

For this purpose, you just have to perform one step before starting Macro recording. Click on the 'Use Relative Reference' under the 'developer' tab. When you will run Macro after saving it, it won't update the same cells again and again. If you don't use the relative approach, then for absolute recording, you don't have to do anything, it automatically does absolute Macro recording. Check out the figure below for further assistance in Relative Macro recording:

Example of Relative Macro recording

The beauty of relative Macro recording is that you can run the Macro anywhere in the sheet, it will execute and show the results in the cells that you have selected(currently).

Here is an example in which we create a Macro in the cells: F6, G6 and H6 and generate the result in some other row or specifically in three cells other than these.

Steps:

1. Go to 'Developer' tab.

2. Under 'Developer' tab, click on 'Use Relative References'.

3. Click on 'Record Macro'.

4. When you click on 'Record Macro', a new window will open as shown in the figure below that will ask you about Macro name and where you want to store the Macro.

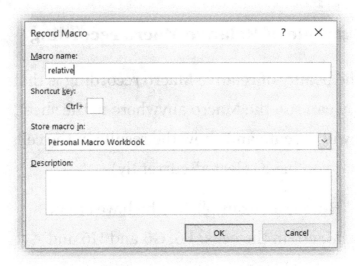

5. Now click on any cells you wish to update and write something in them.

6. We chose the cells 'F6, G6, H6' and wrote something as shown in figure below:

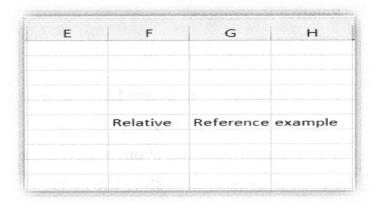

7. After you are done updating cells, click on stop recording. You have successfully saved a relative Macro.

8. Again under 'Developer' tab, click on Macros. A window will open as shown below. Click on run Macro.

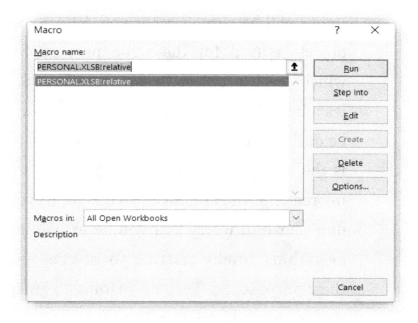

9. It doesn't matter which cell you have selected; three cells will be updated in row with the cell you have selected.

Chapter 6: VBA Excel Objects

If you are familiar with programming languages like Java and C++ then these topics will be very easy for you. VBA Excel object is used for the same purpose for which we use object in Java or C++. So, learning VBA Excel objects for you wouldn't be difficult. The only thing you need to learn is the syntax for calling the objects. As for my readers who are novice to this topic, you don't have to worry as I will be explaining everything briefly relating to objects and their purpose. So, keep on reading to grasp this concept like an expert.

Excel objects

The reason for all the explanation was to help you understand Excel objects properly in an effortless manner. As we said, objects perform some tasks. There are some objects inside Excel that perform tasks that are very useful to us.

Excel is an object too!

As mentioned above objects perform tasks for you. Here, the whole Excel application is an object too. It performs variety of tasks for us. Excel performs tasks like creating graphs or charts, organizing data, providing the ability to users to access Excel file from a range of different device, from different locations!

We also mentioned that an object can contain other objects. Same is the case for Excel. An Excel is an object which contain other objects. We shall present a list four objects that are very popular in Excel. We shall also be explaining in these concepts.

Following is the hierarchy of objects in Excel that a user will deal with, during most of his/her time spent on Excel:

1. Application Objects

2. Workbook Objects

3. Worksheet Objects

4. Range Objects

   (*https://www.tutorialspoint.com/vba/vba_excel_objects.htm*)

All of the objects are under the Application object. To call an object that is under Application object, you have to use '.'. You cannot call an object directly using Application object, you can call it with the reference of previous object which has to be called too.

- To get to a workbook that is named 'workbook' you have to write the following line:

Application.Workbooks("workbook.xlsx")

- Similarly, to open a specific worksheet in a workbook write the following line:

Application.Workbooks("workbook.xlsx").Worksheets(1)

The 1 inside the Worksheets parenthesis is used when there is only one worksheet in a workbook.

- Now suppose you want to retrieve a value from a cell named "B3", then you have to move further down the hierarchy to get this value. You need to write the following line in VBA to access this value:

Application.Workbooks("workbook1.xlsx").Worksheets(1).Range("A1").Value

---

Example of uses of an object

As mentioned earlier, each object has its own methods and properties. The methods are basically the functions which an object performs. Here we will give you an example on how to create a new worksheet in Excel using the object "Worksheets".

Let's create a new worksheet with name : "Hello"

Once inside VBA editor press "Ctrl+G", it will open up an immediate window in which you can start writing VBA code immediately. Write following line:

Worksheets.Add().Name = "Hello"

Now press enter. Go to back to Excel and you will see a new worksheet created under **current** workbook as shown in the screenshot given below

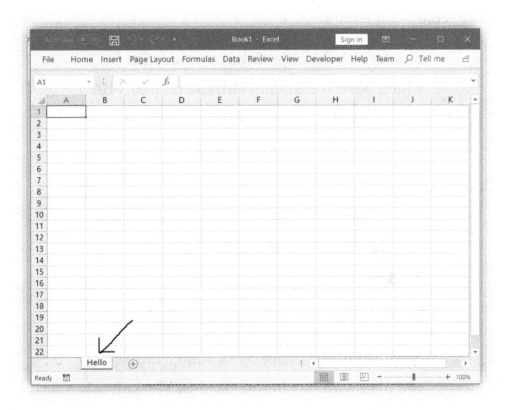

Properties of objects

Every object performs some tasks and each object consists of qualities or attributes that describe what the object is. For example, a car is an object and its properties are engine, color, model etc.

Similarly, VBA objects have properties which describe them. With the help of VBA we can modify the properties of settings. Confusing? This example will clear your concept.

The 'worksheets' object has property 'range' and the range object has the property value, written as:

Worksheets("Book1").Range("A").Value()

Now, value is a property of Range and we can play with its characteristics. You can set the value of a cell using this property and you can display this value in a message box using the function 'MsgBox'.

To display the value, you can write the following code:

Sub **displayValue()**

    Value = Worksheets("book1").Range("A").Value

    MsgBox Value

End **Sub**

Similarly, to set a value of a cell you can write the following code:

Sub **setValue()**

    Worksheets("book1").Range("A").Value = "Set Value"

End **Sub**

In the above example, we used the property value of the Range in two ways:

1. To display the value

2. To set the value of the cell.

Chapter 7: Sending Email from Excel

The topic we are going to discuss in this chapter can be very useful commercially if understood and applied in real-life situations properly. Every one of you must have used email sending and receiving platforms like Yahoo, G-mail, Hotmail, Outlook etc. But, have you used Excel to send email to someone or have you sent bulk of emails to same person at the same time? We assume your answer is :'no'. Well, in this chapter you will be expert in sending bulk of emails to multiple people or even one person.

Again, we will be using Visual Basic to achieve this task. If you have read this book from the very start, by this time you must be completely aware of how important VBA programming in Excel is.

Steps for sending the email

First of all go to 'Developers' tab after opening Excel workbook. Click on Visual Basic. A new window will open. Click on 'Tools' tab inside VBA. Click on references. A new window will be displayed on your screen containing bulks of libraries. Don't be overwhelmed by a large number of libraries. We will use only one of it.

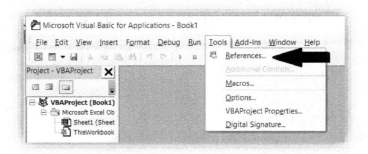

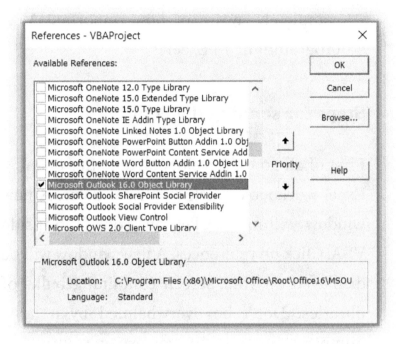

Scroll down the 'References-VBA project' window. You will see a library called Microsoft outlook 16.0(Version as of now) Object Library. Check this Library and click 'Ok'.

Now its time we actually start coding for sending an email to some person/organization.

To do it first of all click on 'Insert ' in VBA window. In the drop-down list click on 'Module'. You have successfully created a module. Now it's time for writing some code!

Inside the Module, type in following code.

```
Sub SendMail()


Dim olApp As Outlook.Application

Dim olMail As Outlook.MailItem


Set olApp = New Outlook.Application

Set olMail = olApp.CreateItem(olMailItem)
```

```
With olMail

    .To = 'abc@gmail.com'

    .Subject = "Message from Excel"

    .Body = "Body of the message"

    .Display

    ' 'olMail.Send

End With

End Sub
```

When you write this code inside VBA and hit run, Excel will take you through a series of steps for configuring the email from which you want to send the email. After that email will be sent to the specific email you typed inside VBA code in front of '.To'.

So, it was easy sending an email through VBA? Sending email to many users is also easy you just add two more lines of code in the above code and Taddaa! Its done.

We need to add a 'loop' to the code. For the readers from 'non-programming' background, loop is just a statement in a code which allows us to execute a specific section of code repeatedly as many time as we like.

Coming back to our topic of sending bulk emails, following changing in the above code can help you send emails to multiple receivers(99 in our case):

```
Sub SendMail()


Dim olApp As Outlook.Application

Dim olMail As Outlook.MailItem


for i=2 To 100

Set olApp = New Outlook.Application

Set olMail = olApp.CreateItem(olMailItem)
```

```
With olMail

    .To = Cells(i,1).Value

    .Subject = Cells(i,2).Value


    .Body = Cells(i,3).Value


    .Display

    ' '.Send

End With

End Sub
```

In the above code we applied **Bold** to some of the text to let you know about the changing or difference between initial code and this code.

Chapter 8: Debugging

As with all the chapters before, we shall begin this chapter by discussing a couple of terminologies. We shall discuss debugging Excel later in this chapter in detail. First of we should know what is debugging and how its effects our coding or to be exact: our computer program. Mind you, the concept of debugging is not limited to Excel. It is applied to almost every program in the computer. Why do we need it? Well, bear with me through this chapter and you will grasp the concept of 'Debugging'.

Debugging

Debugging is the process of removing "bugs" from computer programs that are the reasons for deviation of computer programs from expected behavior.

Bugs
Definition from Wikipedia:

"A software bug is an error, flaw, failure or fault in a computer program or system that causes it to produce an incorrect or unexpected result, or to behave in unintended ways. The process of fixing bugs is termed "debugging" and often uses formal techniques or tools to pinpoint bugs, and since the 1950s, some computer systems have been designed to also deter, detect or auto-correct various computer bugs during operations."

The importance of debugging is obvious from the definitions and explanations of both the "Bugs" and "Debugging". Now, let's jump straight into "debugging in Excel".

Debugging in Excel

The debugger tools in Excel allow us to pause program execution at any stage and then check the value of variables and the continue executing the program. Exciting, Isn't it?

This can be done by using a breakpoint in the program. Setting a breakpoint is very easy and doesn't require any rocket science. All you have to do is to move the cursor to the statement where you want to pause the program's execution and press F9.

Here is an example of simple breakpoint in program:

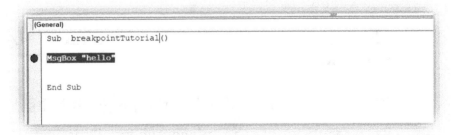

```
(General)
    Sub  breakpointTutorial()
●   MsgBox "hello"

    End Sub
```

The red circle at third line shows that a breakpoint has been set here. When you run the program, the VBA editor halts program execution when it reaches breakpoint. After you have checked your program, to continue the execution, click on small green 'play' button to complete the program's execution and get normal output as always.

You can set the breakpoint of the program in another way, you can write one word in the VBA editor Module to halt programs execution. The word is: 'Stop'. Write this word anywhere in the program where you want to set the breakpoint. When the sequential execution of program will reach this statement, our program will enter into debugging code.

Moving down the code, statement by statement

When you set a breakpoint, the program halts its execution at the place where it is set.

Suppose you want to move through some section of code step by step. This can be done by pressing F8. Each time you press F8, you move to next step. This is very useful and fast way of debugging rather than setting breakpoints at many points in the program!

Conclusion

If you understood the major concepts behind all the chapters in this book, you can call yourself the 'Macro expert'. But we would encourage you to practice the concepts conveyed in this book. By practicing, you will better grasp complex concepts. As they say, 'Practice makes a man perfect'. If you want to make yourself an expert and perfect candidate for 'Excel Macro' jobs then you have to practice the concepts repeatedly to get a strong grip on them.

In this book, we tried our best to explain concepts at the very basic level. The purpose of explaining each and every step at the basic level was to make a layman understand what

Macros are and what are their applications and how to apply them in real life. We tried our best to cover all the major topics regarding 'Excel Macros' in this book.

Welcome to the last page reader, I'm happy to see you here, I hope you had a great time reading my book and if you want to support my work you can share your thoughts and leave a review.

Respectfully,
William B. Skates

9 781792 142840